ABOUT THE AUTHORS

Louise Mullins began her therapeutic career by training as a stress management therapist. She continued to train, and now works as a qualified Psychological Therapist, working with individuals presenting with an array of issues including: relationship problems, low self-esteem, stress, anxiety, depression, grief, bereavement, addiction, abuse, trauma, OCD, phobias, and eating disorders. She specialises in stress related disorders, including Post Traumatic Stress Disorder (PTSD).

Louise uses a humanistic integrative approach to therapy within her private practice. This multi-modal approach combines person-centred, solution focused, transactional, gestalt, interpersonal, psychoanalytic, Cognitive Behavioural, stress management, mindfulness, and psychotherapeutic theories.

Using a holistic approach to therapy, Louise considers the physical, psychological, social and spiritual aspects to an individual's recovery, enabling her to use a combination of therapeutic interventions to suit a client's individual needs, and may combine the use of psychotherapeutic counselling and coaching: A term better known as coach-therapy or personal consultancy.

Louise continues to train within the sphere of Clinical Forensic Psychology, whilst writing. She has authored several best-selling fiction titles within the Psychological Crime Thriller genre. This is her first non-fiction book.

Louise volunteered as an Independent Domestic Violence Advisor (IDVA) for a local charity called SURVIVE. She has also worked as an In-Patient Unit Volunteer (IPUV) for St. Peter's Hospice, and is currently training as a Sex-Offender Treatment Programme worker with the local probation trust, in order to complete an MSc in Forensic Psychology.

Louise has qualifications in the following:
Stress management
Psychotherapeutic Counselling
CBT
Addiction counselling
Domestic abuse
PTSD
Mental health psychology
Forensic psychology
BSc Psychology

Louise Mullins (MNCS)
Psychological Therapist and trainee Clinical Forensic Psychologist.

Sue Mason has recently qualified as a Cognitive Behavioural Therapist. Following ill-health, Sue decided that she would like to channel her passion for achieving good mental health and wellbeing, into working with people suffering with such related issues; coupled with her empathic and compassionate nature, she now feels able to use both her qualifications and experience to help others. Initially, Sue began working with private clients, focusing on aspects such as stress, anxiety, depression, general fatigue and demotivation, OCD and other associated conditions.

However, Sue felt she wanted to help potential health sufferers 'at the source', so she developed a programme for primary school children using CBT techniques, focusing on aspects such as confidence building, self-esteem, positive thinking, mindfulness and more. Sue now presents the programme to year six children, as they prepare to leave primary school and make the transition to secondary school within her locality: She is quite determined to take the programme further afield, in her quest to arm children with tools enabling them to build the foundation for a happy and healthy mental wellbeing into adulthood.

Sue was invited to train to become a facilitator with Macmillan Cancer Support for their HOPE programme. This programme helps cancer patients nearing the end of their treatment, or those that have completed their treatment, and are struggling to regain an element of control over their lives. Sue feels incredibly proud and privileged to be working with some amazing and inspirational people.

Sue Mason (SAC Dip. Cognitive Behavioural Therapy)
Member of BABCP
Cognitive Behavioural Therapist

A NEW THEORY FOR OBSESSIVE THOUGHTS AND COMPULSIVE BEHAVIOURS?

LOUISE MULLINS (MNCS)
AND SUE MASON (MBABCP)

Published in Great Britain in 2015 by New Psychology Press.

This paperback edition published in 2015.

New Psychology Press, Bristol, UK.

ISBN-13: 978-1519432711
ISBN-10: 1519432712

Printed and bound by CreateSpace
www.createspace.com

CONTENTS

DISCLAIMER

Whilst the subject of mental health concerns psychology, neither author professes to be an expert in psychology, of Obsessive Compulsive Disorder (OCD), nor of any other mental health condition. We are exempt from having to request ethical approval from any university, institution or regulating body relating to psychology, for the purposes of research ourselves, because at this time we have only conducted one study, which has been approved by a counselling agency.

We have both studied and practiced differing approaches to the same psychological disorders, and therefore claim only to be qualified through our own individual experiences of working with clients presenting with certain kinds of distress. We do not claim to be qualified practitioner psychologists, and do not claim that our own ideas, thoughts, opinions or practice in relation to our theory, are based on anything more than our own individual professional experiences: And certainly not in opposition to the study, practice, teaching or research already available, relating to our chosen profession.

We do not recommend approaching your own distress, nor do we advocate self-administered treatment for any mental health condition, through the reading of this book alone: We do not condone any practitioner, therapist or otherwise, treating their clients based on any of the ideas from this book, until sufficient research into the theory has been approved for use.

We hope only to engage, inform, and raise debate upon an otherwise silent theoretical approach which could offer an insight into the similarities between many well-recognised mental health conditions; those of obsessive thoughts and compulsive behaviours.

We hope our suggestions within this text will contribute to further teaching, assessment, diagnosis, and treatment for mental health problems, and will be looked upon as a valuable source for future research into these disorders.

We hope that you enjoy the thought-provoking, enlightening, and oftentimes challenging subjects dealt with within this book, and welcome you to take this journey with us using a critical eye.

We ask only that you keep an open mind throughout. We understand the importance of retaining a focus on yourself, whether you are a student, practitioner, teacher, researcher or reader of all things related to the mind, and hope that you begin this journey with us through continued reflexivity - A term which originates from Social Psychology to mean the individual concerned (you), taking note of their own relationship between themselves, others, and the context surrounding them (you, your clients, and your practice). Your own journey is just as (if not more) important than ours, and we hope that whilst reading this book, you consider your own personal and/or professional experiences with mental health, and everything that you have learned/practiced/taught/researched, as well as leaving some room for this new approach. Something we will introduce in the next chapter.

Throughout this book we use abbreviations for Obsessive Compulsive Disorder (OCD), Post-Traumatic Stress Disorder (PTSD), Borderline Personality Disorder (BPD), and Cognitive Behavioural Therapy (CBT). We use the term 'practitioner' to mean anyone qualified to practice therapy (Clinical/Forensic Psychologists, Psychotherapists, Psychiatrists, Counsellors, Coach-Therapists/Personal Consultants, Stress Management Therapists, and hypnotherapists). We use the term 'client' to mean an individual presenting to a practitioner for therapy.

These terms are used in order to make for easy reading.

WHAT ARE OBSESSIVE THOUGHTS AND COMPULSIVE BEHAVIOURS?

When explaining what obsessive thoughts and compulsive behaviours are, it is simple to begin with the well-known condition Obsessive Compulsive Disorder (OCD).

OCD is defined as a mental disorder, characterised by repetitive, obsessive thoughts that in turn lead to compulsive actions. Such thoughts may include feeling compelled to harm others, the necessity for household items to be cleaned repeatedly, and so on. The compulsive actions that result may include hurting another person, excessive cleaning and endless counting.

The disorder itself is well-recognised by mental health professionals, and is included within the Diagnostic and Statistical Manual of Mental Disorders Revision Five (DSM-IV); the British Medical Association (BMA) texts, the National Institute for Clinical Excellence (NICE) guidelines for the approved treatment of mental disorders, and World Health Organisation (WHO) texts. The approved psychotherapeutic treatment for OCD is Cognitive Behavioural Therapy (CBT).

What is possibly harder to express, is the lesser-known fact that OCD is not the only mental health condition which involves obsessive thoughts or compulsive behaviours.

We will now introduce you to some of the other well-known causes of psychological distress in order to illustrate this point.

Firstly, during the rewriting of DSM-V, the practitioners involved in adding and retracting the mental health disorders within the new text, included complicated/prolonged grief as a recognised disorder. Severe grief is defined as an extended period of grief which results from some form of bereavement. This disorder is one of several that was highly debated and criticised after publication; our aim here is not to question if this disorder indeed exists, but to offer our theory as a starting point for discussing how obsessive thoughts and compulsive behaviours fit into this disorder, assuming that they do.

Severe grief includes the obsessive thoughts of loss, or the repeated memory formation of the object/individual of which the bereaved is grieving. This may be the loss of a breast from surviving cancer, the loss of a loved one, or through serious illness, grieving for the person you once were, the necessity to accept that you will never be the same person, in order for you to move on: This is something that acceptance therapy is used for.

Perhaps the individual concerned fears death. The associated compulsive behaviours might be to ensure optimum health so that the grieving individual retains a sense of control over his/her body weight, physical strength, exercise, which therefore offers the individual a sense of control over their own feared death.

We have chosen to use this example first to

ensure that we do not focus entirely on the original idea that OCD is differentiated from other mental health disorders by its two main classifiable symptoms (obsessive thoughts and compulsive behaviours), as we believe that these characteristics are present in many of the known mental health conditions, currently being treated as separate, due to this unrecognised fact.

The second well-known disorder we would like to include is depression. A disorder known by many professionals and sufferers to contain a cycle of negative automatic thinking (I am to blame, I am not worthy of love, etc.), and its associated behaviours (avoiding situations once previously found to be enjoyable, and an inability to raise any level of positivity or excitement towards even the most pleasant of experiences).

In the case of a severely depressed individual who is experiencing suicidal thoughts, the continued envisioning of (and ideas for) ending one's own life, and ideas related thereof, may take up a large amount of the individuals time. Such continued obsessive thoughts can eventually lead to the compulsion for the affected individual to end their life, often to rid themselves of the uncontrollable thought to do so, and not necessarily to conclude their life, and whilst the depressed person may feel an increased level of hopelessness, this person may express that they did indeed wish to purge this sense of harming themselves (Something suicide survivors have expressed).

Furthermore, self-harm is considered a coping mechanism- known to include the obsessive

14

thoughts of harming oneself and the compulsion to do so, which often leaves the individual feeling a sense of relief when they cut or otherwise harm themselves. A form of catharsis only achieved when the individual acts on their thoughts.

Addiction, whether to alcohol, drugs, gambling, shopping, hoarding, pornography or sex, involves the habitual thought of using, followed by the compulsion to use, and which after using, brings about a feeling of relief for the individual. This then becomes a hard-to-break cycle.

It is the same with an individual who has repeatedly committed serious, violent acts. Let's say that this individual committed an offence once every three months before conviction, and that they too have stated that offending acts as a release from the continued obsessional thoughts to harm another person, and that the sense of control and power that is regained after an offence, offers some form of catharsis. We could say that this behaviour is a result of the compulsion to act on those thoughts.

Therefore, could it be possible that obsessive thoughts preclude compulsive behaviours (a habitual action) in several psychological disorders other than OCD?

Firstly, it is rare to find compulsive behaviour present, without the obsessive thoughts leading to such behaviour.

Secondly, it does appear possible that obsessive thoughts and compulsive behaviours, to a certain extent, are present in severe grief, depression, self-harm, addiction, and serial violent offences of a serious nature.

Now, using the idea that obsessive thoughts and compulsive behaviours can be found in many mental health disorders, is it possible that a new theory for obsessive thoughts and compulsive behaviours could offer a fresh insight into the way mental health disorders are approached? The authors of this book hope so.

So how did this theory develop?

Louise Mullins, through her practice and personal interest in mental health psychology and the psychology of offending, developed the idea that in many of the disorders her clients were presenting to therapy with, there seemed to be one commonality that had yet to be explored: That obsessive thoughts tended to be present, in some form or another, within most of the individuals she came into contact with. In addition to this idea, the fact that obsessive thoughts are rarely, if at all, present without leading to some kind of compulsive behaviour, she sought to explore this further by observing the likelihood that her clients showed both obsessive thoughts and compulsive behaviours related to their disorder. To this end, clients were closely observed and monitored, where such characteristics were present. This led her to realise that there may be room for a more holistic approach to the therapeutic process or relationship.

Such an approach, though not as radical as it may at first appear, could afford practitioners a less complex job of teaching, assessing, diagnosing, treating and researching, mental health problems.

To highlight this idea let us begin with a scenario. Case studies are often used within psychology texts to illustrate a way of working with an individual, using a single form of therapy. This is usually to provide the reader with the knowledge of how such a therapy works in practice. Here we aim only to illustrate how phobias also share common characteristics with those of OCD, although the assessment criteria are very different.

We have chosen phobias as these disorders are treated in much the same way as OCD, often using CBT.

Imagine an individual with a severe phobic reaction to spiders. So severe that they may avoid areas where spiders are factually (subjectively) known by the individual to permeate: Such areas may include parks, sheds, and other outside areas.

The thought processes which preclude the associated compulsive behaviours may include, for example: 'There are spiders everywhere', or 'I'll die if a spider comes near me', or 'I won't be able to concentrate on my work if I see one out there.'

The compulsion to ensure they do not come into any contact with the feared insects may involve: systematic checking of vehicles before driving to work, hurried walking through the car-park surrounded by greenland before entering work, and continued agitation which may last several minutes, before the individual feels able to settle down and start work inside the building.

Such obsessive thoughts and compulsive behaviours are a direct result of a sense of threat or a deep-routed fear, which may have resulted from a traumatic incident when the individual came into contact with a spider years before. Or, as is often the case, it is just an evolutionary response. A primal affect that as a species they no longer need, but as it is biological, and quite possibly a conditioned response to threat, these reactions are automatic, and therefore this person does not make conscious (appropriate) decisions when in close proximity to a spider.

The thought process, emotional response and compulsive behaviour towards spiders have a cause and effect. A natural fear response similar to that of the fight, flight or freeze response - the well-known in-built perception of a harmful event.

As we have previously suggested, it is easy to begin with OCD, but if we look closely at the thought-behaviour processes involved, there are many similarities between this disorder and others.

What we suggest is nothing exceptional or 'new,' in that we are not proposing that the teaching, assessment, diagnosis, treatment or research of any mental health disorder which may include obsessive thoughts and compulsive behaviours be altered or that they be treated with caution. We do not question the reliability of current research, nor any of the NICE (National Institute for Clinical Excellence) approved, psychotherapeutic interventions (often CBT) for the current disorders that they claim to work well for. However we suggest that this theory compliments the use of CBT as a recommended intervention.

Though neither author suggests CBT works for everything, there has been a definite increase in its use for various mental health conditions in the past five years. What we propose could offer another reason for the effectiveness of CBT as a form of therapeutic intervention. In fact we consider that CBT may work well because it is being both consciously used to challenge negative thinking and behaviour, and unconsciously it is also working to challenge obsessive thinking and compulsive behaviour. Something we believe neither practitioners nor clients are aware of.

Could the usefulness of CBT for many well-recognised mental health disorders, be less to do with the Improving Access to Psychological Therapies (IAPT) initiative, the relationship between the therapist and his/her client, or the way in which CBT works on the cognitive processes in individuals (a mode of medicalised psychological intervention which works on the brain (thoughts), feelings (emotions), and behaviours (body)), and more to do with the fact that it alters obsessive thinking and compulsive behaviour in some way?

CBT is perhaps one of the most holistic approaches to mental health disorders used to date, in that it works on the individual's cognitions (brain/mind), and physical actions (behaviour), and requires consideration of support networks, work-home life balance, hobbies, and an individual's beliefs, both positive and negative (and sometimes spiritual) aspects of themselves.

We do not wish to begin a lengthy debate about the personal (physical and psychological), social, and spiritual possibilities of this form of therapy. But we would like to include this information here, so that you can see how fitting this form of therapeutic intervention is for many individuals in the treatment of many psychological disorders.

We are asking however, the questions that have yet to be asked.

Are we treating obsessive thoughts and compulsive behaviours when using CBT, or are we only dealing with the thought-emotion-behaviour processes that current theories suggest?

Why does CBT work so well with an array of different clients, presenting with varied degrees of differing mental health difficulties, resulting from many different causes of distress?

The aim of this book is to bring to light a new theory for inclusion within texts which address the theoretical causes for, characteristics of, and approaches to, mental health problems. We are suggesting that what we are doing already is working well and should continue, but that it is perhaps not efficiently working only for the reasons we thought it was. That is that CBT may have multiple reasons for its effectiveness. Current evidence only offers us one theory: We propose a second.

Before we continue, please consider what you already know about obsessive thoughts and compulsive behaviours, (perhaps some information you have read or heard relating to OCD). We would advise you to try to remain objective throughout the following chapters.

We hope that you enjoy this short journey with us, and begin to question whether our proposal does require further study. Could the knowledge we have so far produced, offer an invaluable theory to the arena of mental health, and the practice of CBT?

In answering the question posed at the beginning of this chapter, we would like to conclude by stating that obsessive thinking and compulsive behaviours are perhaps present in most psychological disorders. We state this with caution because, of course, this is something that requires further investigation.

THEORIES OF OBSESSION AND COMPULSION

As with all theories, those of OCD alter according to the time and place in which they are developed. Theories are, in essence, historically, socially and culturally constructed. They are based on the assumptions and experiences of those individuals (both personal and professional) who develop them. They require vigorous testing as to their reality and effectiveness, and they are used to form the methods (approaches) of treatment (modes of therapeutic intervention) for the disorders they are aimed at treating.

Theories on the causes of OCD began around 300 years ago with the belief that distorted religious experience was to blame.

Feelings of grandiosity (now seen as a characteristic of bipolar disorder), and deeply felt religious experience, as well as renouncing God, were believed to be the causes of over-thinking (ruminating - now a diagnosable characteristic of depression) and carefully considered actions (now a well-recognised criteria for the diagnosis of anxiety or PTSD).

When psychoanalytic theorists began to dominate psychology, the therapeutic interventions believed to aid hysteria and melancholy - now better known as bipolar and unipolar depression - were often painful (Electro-Convulsive Therapy (ECT)), arose from no research (hot and cold compresses placed on exposed areas of the body) or dangerous (blood-letting - using a syringe to take copious amounts of blood from a patient's veins).

The psychoanalysts who developed such theories and approaches to the treatment of mental health problems, then sought to consider the causes of OCD.

What they believed to be the route cause was doubt and indecisiveness. Or as the French writer Pierre Janet inferred, 'loss of will and low mental energy' (cited by Goodman, 2013)

The symbolic meaning of the obsession and the grooming/hoarding that appeared present with many patients presenting with OCD type behaviours during this time, took precedence over the original idea that distorted religious experience was the cause.

In contrast to psychoanalysis, CBT derived from Rational Emotive Behaviour Therapy (REBT), and the learning theory model of behaviour which derived from psychology has now taken precedence over the psychoanalytical approach to OCD.

Behaviour Therapy is theoretically underpinned by the idea that 'obsessions and compulsions are the result of abnormal learned responses and actions' (Goodman, W. 2013). In simplified terms; a neutral object is associated with fear through negative conditioning.

We do not intend to contradict such theories, nor do we wish to criticise their origin. What we do hope however, is that such theories for OCD, and the treatments used for individuals exhibiting this disorder (CBT), are considered to be beneficial for more than the obvious reason - that they work by altering deeply ingrained beliefs over particular events, resulting in the affected individual accommodating their behaviour to their associated feelings over such an event.

What we would like to consider is whether CBT, which is widely used for stress, anxiety, depression, PTSD, addiction, eating disorders, OCD, and phobias, works because it directly alleviates the obsessive thoughts and compulsive behaviours present within these disorders. And not just the negative thinking patterns, but also the associated emotions resulting from them; as well as the compulsion to rid the anxiety-provoking thoughts with a habitual action, as all of the current literature on CBT suggests.

What we propose is that CBT works for possibly a different reason than it is said to do so for OCD, as well as for many other mental health problems.

So how does CBT work on obsessive thinking and compulsive behaviour?

Perhaps because negative thinking patterns are present within many disorders of the mind (think schizophrenia, bipolar, and Borderline Personality Disorder (BPD)), the one-to-one sessions with a therapist, the self-administered homework afterwards, and the motivation to believe that change is possible, enables the tools of the trade to work well. But, imagine that hidden beneath the inner workings of the theory, that by altering the way we think about a person, event or situation, can in turn change the way we feel about such things, and thus enable us to behave in a more 'positive' way despite these oppositional life adversities. This therefore could encompass these subtle changes to our obsessional thoughts, which in turn alters our compulsive behaviour.

Is this a result of CBT that has yet to be investigated?

We think so.

So how could current theories of obsessive thoughts and compulsive behaviours be altered to accommodate this new knowledge, and how could this information assist individuals living with other mental health conditions?

The truth is, somebody has already laid the foundations for such a theory.

Dr Benjamin Greenberg, a Brown University psychiatrist, has been studying the use of Deep Brain Stimulation for individuals who show severe symptoms of OCD.

DBS (as it is termed), works by stimulating certain areas of the brain using millimetre thick, nylon fibres inserted into the brain (probes). A device similar to a pacemaker is surgically implanted over those areas of the brain associated with regulating thoughts and behaviour; a regular surgical procedure to insert the fibres and stimulate these neurological pathways, has been found to result in almost all symptoms being physically disabled. There was a '25% reduction in the symptoms that 73% of the participants of the study rated, three years later' (Greenberg, 2013).

The method is still in its infancy and is used only in sufferers who display the most severe characteristics of the disorder and who agree to take part in the study for outcome measures, but it does look promising.

What is of interest, are not the methods used, or their effectiveness, but the theory used to develop the study.

Dr Greenberg has developed a theory, not dissimilar to our own, in order to explain OCD. It does not defy the idea that cognitive distortions (negative thought processes) and compulsive behaviours characterise OCD from other mental health disorders. In fact it adds to it, just as we hope to.

Although his approach does not consider any mental health problems other than OCD and addiction, he sees the comparison that addictive thinking and behaviour has with the characteristics of OCD, and believes addiction to be worthy of inclusion in his theory.

He also advocates the use of psychotherapeutic interventions such as CBT to cure the characteristics that addiction and OCD share. He is, however, one of the first contemporary theorists and practitioners, to see the other possible benefits CBT has to offer the treatment of mental health issues, other than OCD, that target only obsessive thoughts and compulsive behaviours.

Dr Greenberg's theory is based on the notion of the existence of 'Habitual Behaviour Disorder' (Greenberg, 2013).

He sees the traits of addiction as closely resembling those of OCD. For instance, addiction is goal-directed, in that the individual psychologically craves their addiction of choice (drugs, alcohol, gambling, shopping, hoarding, pornography or sex). He also sees the commonalities that addictive behaviour has with the behaviours of individuals with a diagnosis of OCD: That of habitual behaviour.

With regard to OCD, he suggests that the obsession leads to the compulsion, which again becomes a habitual behaviour, and not the other way around: This supports current theories as to how CBT works. By combating negative thoughts, it is possible to positively alter the associated negative behaviour.

When the goals change, with OCD or addiction, there becomes an avoidance of change (when the amount of heroin taken needs to be increased in order to feel the same effect, it becomes more difficult to stop taking it). This perpetual cycle of drug taking, or in relation to OCD, cleaning perhaps, becomes a hard habit to break.

When Louise first encountered Dr Greenberg's idea she considered her previous observations with clients who entered her practice and questioned whether habitual behaviour disorder could be used to explain other mental health conditions. She asked: *Are obsessions and compulsions present in any psychological disorders, other than OCD and addiction?* It appeared so; and it didn't take very long to consider the possibility that indeed they are.

Coming from a psychology background, as a specialist in stress and trauma, she sought to find out whether the associated symptoms of PTSD (rumination, intrusive thoughts, avoidance behaviours, decreased self-esteem, depression and apathy) could highlight the occurrence of obsessive thinking and compulsive behaviours in her clients.

Rather than researching the phenomenon on anonymous participants, she closely observed the precedence of such characteristics in her own clients, presenting with a diagnosis of PTSD.

Her findings matched recorded data which suggests that many, but not all, individuals who seek therapy with a diagnosis of PTSD have previously experienced some form of abuse. Of most abuse survivors who attend therapy, almost all have a current or prior addiction to something. All of the individuals, with a diagnosis of PTSD, attending Louise's practice during this time, exhibited obsessive thoughts and compulsive behaviours.

This phenomenon is not unusual, as the diagnostic criteria for PTSD, as previously mentioned, includes rumination, intrusive thoughts and avoidance behaviours.

Using this as a basis, Louise sought to find any data relating these characteristics of PTSD to any other psychological disorder other than OCD, and as Dr Greenberg suggests, addiction. No literature for prior or current studies could be found at the time.

As Louise is currently training within Clinical Forensic Psychology, and has a personal interest in the use of CBT within forensic settings (often termed forensic CBT), she wondered if there had been, or was any current research being undertaken, into the obsessive thoughts and compulsive behaviours of offenders. Wondering if offenders of serial violent crimes such as rape or murder had expressed, during psychological assessment, obsessive thinking and compulsive behaviour to rationalise their acts. Again, there was none.

She then reflected on evidence which suggests that perhaps certain crimes (often considered to be compulsive) such as non-sexual related serial murder, could be the result of obsessive thinking and compulsive behaviours more so than the research literature suggests (that power, control, or catharsis cause such violent acts in individuals already predisposed to display such behaviours). There is no such recorded data concerning obsessive thoughts or compulsive behaviour as a possible link to individuals exhibiting serial violent tendencies.

Let us return for one moment to OCD, and consider this as a further basis to demonstrate our theory.

Scans have revealed that individuals with a diagnosis of OCD show heightened activation (hyper-activated) within certain brain areas. Such brain changes, which have been stimulated using Dr Greenberg's pioneering technique of Deep Brain Stimulation, show similar characteristics to the brain areas known to show higher levels of activation in serial violent offenders.

If CBT, which is a therapeutic intervention that can alleviate the symptoms of OCD and many other mental health problems, works by enabling the sufferer to deconstruct and reconstruct their negative thoughts into more positive appraisals, altering their actions so that they are no longer harmful to their psychological health, could it be used in much the same way if it were targeting habitual behaviour disorder, as Dr Greenberg suggests?

If we consider serial violent offending to be a disorder in itself, then yes, it can be. CBT is now used widely within the psychological services available within prisons. But for all kinds of reasons, forensic CBT has never been considered for use specifically with serial violent offenders, in order to target obsessive thoughts or compulsive behaviours.

If Dr Greenberg's theory aids our understanding of obsessive thoughts and compulsive behaviours in addiction, then could ours offer further knowledge into the effectiveness of forensic CBT with this particular client?

Possibly.

If CBT works to alleviate the symptoms of several mental health disorders, something most other approaches do not, could it be working for several different reasons?

Possibly.

To clarify this point, let's consider person-centred (humanistic) counselling, which tends to work very well for clients presenting with long-term problems or deep-rooted issues (depression, abuse etc.).

CBT is just as effective for treating depression and the associated symptoms of abuse present in PTSD, as is person-centred counselling.

So how is it that when treating the same characteristics present within two diagnosable disorders, the diagnostic criteria are very different?

We do not wish to engage in a debate on the medicalisation of human distress here, this book is too short. What we do however note, is that if there is a possible link between disorders by two verifiable characteristics (obsessive thoughts and compulsive behaviours) why has this area not already been investigated, and why has this question not been addressed before?

We, as yet, do not know the answers; although, perhaps we could consider these questions further ourselves.

If practitioners were to treat the symptoms and not the causes of distress, therapy would not work at all. But, both person-centred and CBT approaches work in different ways, to different degrees, and take different durations for a noticeable effect to appear.

Person-centred counselling seeks to find the root cause of an individual's distress, through rapport building with the client, active and empathic listening, paraphrasing, summarising and feedback. CBT seeks to do so through challenging an individual's negative thought processes and offering suggestions for behaviour change. In an indirect way, and often through months of therapy, the client attending person-centred counselling will delve into the root cause of their distress. Whereas in just eight to twelve sessions (two or three months), the client attending CBT will be directed to do the same.

Could this be because CBT treats the cause (event) and symptoms (diagnosable characteristics) through questioning the reliability of the associated disordered thought processes, and habitual behaviours of the condition? Or is it because it is partly doing this, and partly targeting the obsessive thoughts and compulsive behaviours of the individual? Something that does not appear to occur within person-centred counselling; and how could this phenomenon have by-passed all previous and current literature relating to psychological distress?

In the next chapter, we highlight the possibility that assessment during the initial consultation could give the opportunity to diagnose disorders, and develop an appropriate treatment plan for individuals presenting with obsessive thoughts and compulsive behaviours. After all, if nobody is aware that the symptoms exist, it is difficult to assess them, to develop a theory for their cause, build an appropriate therapeutic approach to treat them, research the phenomenon, and teach others about its presence.

Put simply, if nobody has been looking for an alternative reason behind an individual's thinking, and subsequent behaviour change when CBT is being used, then nobody will know it exists, and therefore nobody will have a reason to study it. We will remain ignorant of its presence and its affect.

We consider the process of assessment as an important area in which to investigate the possibility of obsessive thoughts and compulsive behaviours as characteristics of an individual's psychological disorder (diagnosis).

We do not consider assessment to be the most important part of therapeutic practice, but it is necessary, and the consulting room is the easiest place to begin: Possibly because it enables the client to have their say, before the process of therapy begins, and because it is possible to include obsessive thoughts and compulsive behaviours within the client case notes/sheets/history/checklist.

If such questions were considered before therapy began, practitioners would be able to assess their prevalence from the start of the therapeutic encounter. Although this would need to be approached with caution as there is the possibility of bias, if you are seeking a certain behaviour or particular thinking style in your client, you will see it.

Therefore we consider assessment to be an opportunistic, but not necessary, place to establish such characteristics of obsessive thoughts and compulsive behaviours in our clients.

ASSESSMENT

If we were to assess an individual before considering the appropriate therapeutic intervention, would we change the way that it is currently done?

The short answer is 'no'.

If we were to consider how to effectively respond to *all* individuals, whatever the issue they present with, would we use the same approach to treatment?

Again, the answer is 'no'.

So why then, is CBT used as a cure-all in this current climate?

The answer is, because it works.

It is cost effective, short-term (most clients attend eight to twelve sessions once weekly), and long-acting. That is, it is an intervention which enables the client to learn, practice, and continue the techniques themselves, long after therapy has ended.

It is extremely commonplace whilst undertaking CBT, that the therapist will present the client with homework based upon what has been discussed throughout the particular session – this is proven to be a vital part of the therapeutic relationship. Thus the individual coaches themselves throughout their lives, using the same techniques for their current (and subsequent) issues which may develop in the future. It is a programme of recovery that can be used time and again. It is also one of the only known therapeutic interventions which can be utilised by the client, for themselves.

What if we could use a slightly altered version of CBT for several mental health disorders?

We could, and we do.

CBT is used alongside Eye-Movement Desensitisation and Reprogramming (EMDR) for trauma survivors, and those exhibiting the symptoms of PTSD (rumination, intrusive thoughts, flashbacks, nightmares, panic attacks, and avoidance behaviour). It is used in coaching (personal, health, business), and can be used alongside other therapeutic modalities (person-centred counselling, family counselling, interpersonal counselling, addiction counselling, stress management, and mindfulness).

CBT is also, in itself, a secondary approach, having originated from (REBT) and the learning theory model of behaviour; something which itself was derived from social learning theory (the idea that we learn how to behave by witnessing other individuals), also known as conditioning. So could CBT be used to form its own model of therapy? Enabling it to work solely on obsessive thinking and compulsive behaviours?

It could be.

What if to promote our theories we, like many theorists, came up with a brilliant name for the condition which has for so long characterised itself in many different ways for years through: stress, anxiety, depression, severe grief, PTSD, addiction, self-harm, serial violent offences, OCD, phobias, eating disorders, bipolar, schizophrenia, and BPD?

We have.

We term this, our theory, Cognitive Behavioural Disorder.

DIAGNOSIS

Firstly, let us tell you that we are not taking a light-hearted approach to the development of this theory.

Neither do we criticise the way in which mental health is taught, assessed, diagnosed, treated or researched. What we are doing however, is demonstrating how difficult it is in contemporary Britain to develop a theory, and offer a solution to treating a mental health condition, especially when your idea has little evidence to support it.

Whilst we condone the vigorous testing of new approaches to mental health disorders, and their treatments, we understand how difficult it is in this climate, to have your voice heard. This is especially so when you are effectively adding knowledge to an otherwise already well-lead area, such as mental health.

What is usually required is a post-graduate qualification in Clinical Psychology/Psychiatry/Psychotherapy, and/or to be of the male sex: Neither author is.

This is not a sexist comment. It is a fact that there are more white males in all areas of science (including psychology), than those of the female gender, or of other ethnic backgrounds.

What we are able to produce however, are both of the recommended skills: A working title for our theory (A New Theory for Obsessive Thoughts and Compulsive Behaviours?), and a name for the phenomenon that we propose requires further study to either support or condemn our theory; namely Cognitive Behavioural Disorder.

CBD (as we shall from now on term it), is characterised by three criteria, which we would expect to be evident in any individual exhibiting the disorder.

Firstly there will be obsessive thoughts. Secondly there will be compulsive behaviours. Thirdly there will be a diagnosis of at least one mental health condition, which may or may not have been previously mentioned within the preceding chapters of this book.

We estimate that if one in four individuals in the world, according to statistics, suffer from some kind of mental health problem at least once in their life-time - should our theory be supported by evidence, that it is possible that one quarter of the world's population is suffering from Cognitive Behavioural Disorder right now,

We are merely highlighting the precedence of mental health issues here, not providing the reader with a definite reason for taking this theory seriously - at least not at this stage.

But think about it. What if this theory were researched? What if mental health professionals became aware of the information we provide within this book?

We invite you to question what we are saying. Does this theory contrast, contradict or compliment the literature already published in relation to the causes of, theories for, and the approaches used to treat mental health disorders?

We hope to raise debate, challenge your views, and create a starting point for future research into this phenomenon.

Diagnosis itself cannot provide a definitive answer to the question 'what works in mental health?', but by considering the fact that this theory shows the commonalities between the many diagnosable mental health conditions that exist, and is treatable in the same way it is currently being treated (using CBT-based techniques), means that the teaching, assessment, diagnosis, treatment, and research of Cognitive Behavioural Disorder will continue just as it is now.

We are merely adding a new piece of information that we feel hasn't yet been explored.

So how will this disorder be treated?

In the next chapter we examine how CBT works and why: And whether or not CBT (as it is currently practiced) could be used to treat CBD.

TREATMENT

CBT is an approved and highly recommended form of psychotherapeutic intervention for many mental health disorders. It is inexpensive, its techniques are easily learned and utilised, and it is well-recognised.

The basic toolkit for CBT is a good therapist (one with relevant qualifications, understanding, and experience working with the approach), and a client.

CBT works on the principle that, the way we think can affect our feelings, and consequently our behaviour. The theory derives from psychology, as well as 'learning' and 'social learning' models of behaviour.

Cognitive psychologists have bridged the gap between our understanding of the brain and behaviour.

Cognitive processes inform what is fed into our brain, through our interaction with the world around us, including other people. Our brain and mind are linked through conscious and unconscious processing of our wider surroundings. And yet, it too alters according to the information we give out to the world. Put simply, our brains and our behaviour are linked by learning more about the world. We also offer the world further information about ourselves which is then processed by others in that world. We feed and are fed by action and reaction.

If we return to CBT as a therapeutic approach to

distorted thinking patterns, and the subsequent actions and reactions of them, just as 'learning' is the gap between brain and behaviour, 'feelings' are the gap between thoughts and behaviour. The mind (psychology/consciousness/feelings) is the 'gap' that cognitive psychologists have filled with decades of dedicated research into the link between body (brain), and behaviour (actions/reactions).

CBT works to fill the void that the client may have, in understanding that it is their feelings that link their thoughts to their behaviour.

Take for example a child who whilst walking one day, is bitten by a dog. This incident is the event. Years later, that child (now an adult) is confronted by a vicious looking dog. The original reaction to the event (fear, anger, hostility) returns. The adult decides that today they don't need to walk through the park (the quickest way to work) and walks another way. Now consider that this avoidance of a specific threat (the dog) becomes a habitual action.

Of course our brains are incredibly complex, and have the capacity to retain the thoughts, feelings and behaviours we experience throughout our lives. Our brains have an ability to recall situations we have experienced, and react in a similar fashion to the way we did when the original event occurred.

Consider that this adult has been obsessing over another possible dog attack for several years, taking longer and longer to get to work, avoiding anywhere and everywhere they may come into contact with a dog, to the detriment of career, relationship (his partner may find it difficult to understand, leading to arguments over an inability to take the children to the park), and also emotional health.

The adult contacts a therapist who decides to approach this phobic reaction to the past trauma (the event) with CBT. How does he go about it?

In ten sessions the clients negative thinking patterns are highlighted, paraphrased, and homework is provided to challenge his behaviour. On entering a park, this person must be with somebody. Next they must enter alone. Next they must deliberately walk near a dog; then invite the dog over, and so on, until the person feels comfortable enough to approach a large dog and offer the dog a treat.

This form of therapy involves altering negative thought processes as well as taking part in activities designed to challenge his habitual behaviours of avoidance whilst learning how to act in a more positive, socially acceptable way to his feelings.

Now consider how CBT is used to combat OCD.

The client's negative thought processes are challenged through therapy, and they are given homework (to write down how they feel before they cleans their hands for the fifth time, or perhaps to leave one number out of their habitual counting routine, and note down what happened afterwards).

What if we were treating obsessive thoughts and compulsive behaviours?

We would use the same approach to CBD as we have done with the dog phobia and OCD.

So could an approach to treating CBD be beneficially renamed?

Such a debate is worth entering into for several

reasons.

In order for there to be a teachable, diagnosable, assessable and researchable disorder, there must always be a form of therapeutic intervention which deals specifically with that disorder.

If we (the authors) were treating an individual diagnosed with OCD, we would have the appropriate tools lined-up in order to work with that disorder (CBT for OCD).

Now consider that we were treating depression, again, we would work with the individual using CBT for depression.

So, if we were to approach treating a client specifically for their obsessive thoughts and compulsive behaviours, not necessarily presenting to us with a diagnosis of OCD or depression, would we use either of those methods?

No: But, we might be forced to. Why? Because there is no current method approved for use specifically with these characteristics alone.

This is why we have considered the possibility of an intervention aimed specifically for the treatment of CBD. We have considered that this should be named Cognitive Behavioural Disorder Therapy (CBDT). And we propose that both the prevalence of CBD in individuals, and the possibility of treating the disorder (currently undiagnosed), is investigated further in the next chapter.

RESEARCH

Most of the available literature describes obsessive thoughts and compulsive behaviours as being a characteristic of OCD only. Dr Greenberg's theory of habitual behaviour disorder suggests that such characteristics also define addiction. What we are suggesting is that obsessive thoughts and compulsive behaviour may characterise other mental health conditions too.

Much research has been focused on the understanding of the causes of mental ill health. It is now a mandatory part of the curriculum for the undergraduate study of psychology, for instance, to consider a bio-psychosocial approach to mental health. This is a holistic approach which takes into consideration an individual's biological predisposition to mental illness, their psychology, and their socio-economic background.

Let us consider for a moment the diagnostic criteria for personality disorders (We choose psychopathic personality disorder to illustrate our point; not because we consider psychopathic traits to be of more importance).

With regard to Psychopathic Personality Disorder (PPD), there are several diagnostic criteria (characteristics) that are assessed.

Firstly, an individual must exhibit the following, in order for a diagnosis to be made: controlling behaviour, manipulative behaviour, a lack of empathy (no remorse), a lack of emotional intelligence (mimicking rather than feeling emotions), and distorted psychological regulation (impulsive or compulsive behaviour). All of these characteristics are behaviours. This is because it is difficult to assess the subjective (thoughts, ideas, emotions) feelings of an individual who finds it difficult to act mindfully (consider their feelings before acting or express their emotions).

Secondly, individuals with a diagnosis of PPD are slightly more likely to commit crime. Such individuals within the prison system are assessed by forensic and clinical psychologists, just as repeat and serious offenders are, in order to ascertain whether or not they pose a risk to themselves or the public, and to assess the likelihood of them committing an offence once they are released.

Risk assessments, as well as psychological assessments, are undertaken by psychologists within forensic settings, and the reported findings of research derived from this information, suggests several important points: childhood trauma (abuse), life adversity, and addiction are prevalent in almost all offenders with a diagnosis of PPD.

There is however, one important piece of information that has yet to be researched, and that is the presence of obsessive thoughts and compulsive behaviours, which we consider may be evident in repeat offenders with a diagnosis of PPD.

Let us consider for a moment the use of CBT within forensic settings (prison, Offender Treatment Programmes (OTP), psychiatric hospitals etc.), and look at how it is used in treating individuals with a diagnosis of PPD.

Psychologists and psychotherapists working with offenders within a forensic setting, use a slightly different variation of CBT, focusing specifically on challenging negative thinking patterns, as it is often more difficult to offer homework for such clients within a prison or hospital environment. Such practitioners, just as other therapists do in other settings, will work with the client to discover the root cause of their distress, as well as the negative thought processes related to the event, the goal being to alter the client's inappropriate behaviours.

These clients may also present with issues such as addiction, stress, depression, suicidal ideation, and abuse. All of which, as previously suggested, may involve continual (obsessive) negative thinking and habitual (compulsive) behaviours.

What if we were to focus on only the obsessive thoughts and compulsive behaviours that such an individual presents with?

This would encompass all of the associated mental health issues (addiction, stress, depression, suicidal ideation, and abuse) as well as the negative thinking which leads to the compulsion to use drugs, self-harm, become aggressive, violent, or commit a crime.

We would still be able to discover the cause for the Cognitive Behaviour Disorder (abuse), then challenge the behaviours which result from the cause (addiction), and seek to address the symptoms these issues create in themselves (stress, depression, self-harm, aggression/violence, offending), but we would be focusing on the obsessive thoughts and compulsive behaviours surrounding these issues:

Something that treats both the individual's issues as a whole (holistically), and seeks to address such issues in a short time frame - Something that single-session CBT and Solution Focused Therapy (SFT) already does.

Let's pause for thought here, and consider another possible benefit that such in intervention may have. There is a saying, well-known in addiction recovery programmes - including Alcoholics Anonymous - that a habit takes ninety days to form and ninety days to change.

Wouldn't it be wonderful, if we could treat an individual presenting with CBD characteristics within three months (ninety days), whatever their current diagnoses?

We will offer you one more example of CBT being used within a forensic setting in order to clarify the points we have raised within this chapter, before moving on to explain the need for further research in this area.

Imagine you are a therapist working within a prison, and that the next client to walk into your consulting room is an individual who has been sentenced to life in prison for serial murder.

As part of a psychological assessment, when this person is asked to express if they feel comfortable with their feelings in any way, prior to or after the offence, they tell you this:-

That the first time they offended (the event) they were angry: Afterwards they were not. For the first time in years they felt a sense of relief. After several weeks they began to ruminate on the event (the murder). They remember the event, imagining that it was happening again. They could smell the victim's fear; could taste the change in the atmosphere; could picture every detail of the event, as if they had gone back to that place and time. The memories are so strong that they began to feel the adrenaline pumping through their body; the feeling of being once again powerful and in control, in what they termed their otherwise frustrating, dull life, reminding them of the original event.

They would wake up each day and leave for work, but often, without prompting, the images (flashbacks) and thoughts would resurface. Thoughts of violence may take up a lot of time. Eventually this leads to a compulsion to kill. And several months after the original event, they murder again.

The act itself dampened obsessive thoughts and enabled a sense of catharsis: But not for long, because this individual killed several times over a number of years. And each time they stated that not only did the act offer a sense of calm, but it also overcame the obsessive thoughts and compulsion to kill, for several weeks.

It is obvious here that there is more to the offence than a past or current psychology. The individual was not acting on impulses that suddenly graduated from nothing. There is no mental health diagnosis. This is not a psychopath. This is an intelligent individual who cannot control their urges.

There is a build-up which leads to the person feeling like a simmering pot before the crescendo (event). This may have been suppressed for years by addiction, aggressive/violent serial offending or even OCD (behaviours which result from disordered thinking).

However these urges had been controlled for the previous thirty years, the coping mechanisms no longer worked. They wore off. Perhaps the person lost their job or their relationship (somebody who had previously satiated the predisposition to offend) ended: Either way, there has been a 'battle' with the obsessive thoughts and compulsive behaviours that (we suggest) are a disorder in themselves.

Perhaps addiction, aggressive/violent serial offending or even OCD are simply symptoms of these characteristics. After all, these are behavioural disorders, and have a biological, psychological or social cause - they are a combination of nature (biology) and nurture (environment).

But just as these characteristics are quantifiable, are obsessive thoughts and compulsive behaviour?

That is something we wanted to find out.

Current literature on obsessive thoughts and compulsive behaviours tends to focus on the biological causes of OCD. The individual's serotonin levels within the brain (biology); The individual's history and thinking style (psychology); Their behaviour patterns and their relationship with others (social self). What is not questioned is whether their cognitive processes alone, are causing these behaviours. Even though both pharmacological (medical interventions) and psychological treatments (psychotherapy) seek to address the biological and psychological causes of psychological disorders.

Medical treatment for OCD may, at the lowest level of present symptoms, involve a prescribed dose of anti-depressants known as Selective Serotonin Re-uptake Inhibitors. These work on regulating the levels of serotonin within the affected individual's brain. In severe cases, as we have already described, Deep Brain Stimulation may be used.

The main psychological treatment for OCD is CBT, which works on challenging the individuals negative thought patters and behaviours.

Therefore we suggest that CBT, currently used for many mental health issues, is working. But not only on the negative thinking styles and behaviours of the individual. Psychologists have stated that often therapy is more effective when the client/patient undertakes a course of anti-depressant treatment; thus, one intervention compliments the other.

The cognitive process of thinking is too complex for us to include within this chapter, but if we think of cognition as a process involving the brain (biology) and the mind (psychology) of an individual, and their behaviour as being a result of their cognitions (which CBT seeks to address), we can better understand how CBT might also help to alleviate obsessive thoughts and compulsive behaviours.

If an individual's cognitive processes are disturbed, and their behaviours affected by this disturbance, then we can see how a theory for Cognitive Behavioural Disorder may operate within many of the diagnostic categories, currently accepted for mental health disorders.

Such diagnostic categories include:

Stress, anxiety, unipolar and bipolar depression, severe grief disorder, addiction, PTSD, OCD, phobias, self-harming, suicidal ideation, BPD, PPD, serial violent offending (rape/murder), and ADHD (a subject we will visit shortly).

We recommend that future research is undertaken to incorporate only the obsessive thoughts and compulsive behaviours present in an individual with a current diagnosis of a psychological disorder. We also suggest that both quantitative (statistical measures) and qualitative (interviewing, self-reports) methods are used to study the phenomenon. This will ensure that any individuals participating in the study are able to offer their own subjective view on themselves and 'their' disorder, as well as testing the presence of obsessive thinking and compulsive behaviour; rather than focusing on their condition (depression, addiction etc.) or the causes of the symptoms they present with (abuse, adversity etc.).

Such measures will ensure that we are not biased in our view for seeking a definitive answer to the question we pose:

Are obsessive thoughts and compulsive behaviours present within this individual's disorder?

Another idea might be to guard against the influence a diagnosis may have on the researcher's investigation, by investigating the phenomenon 'blindly'. That is, that the researcher will only know that participants have a diagnosis, but not what that diagnosis is.

Research should be grounded, but not limited to, the theory of Cognitive Behaviour Disorder.

In order to argue for the relevance of this theory, we should seek literature based on Habitual Behaviour Disorder and any relevant papers relating to the study of the thought processes involved in compulsive behaviour. Whether such theories are aimed at OCD or addiction is irrelevant, as we believe that obsessive thoughts and compulsive behaviours are already present in these disorders.

We hope to question the effectiveness of our theory by comparing it to other approaches, just as all psychological theories and methods are.

In the following chapter we consider what this suggested approach to obsessive thoughts and compulsive behaviours could provide to the future study of mental health problems.

Whether through studying, teaching, theory, method, assessment, diagnosis, treatment or research, we hope to provide practitioners in the field, and clients alike, with the knowledge of this phenomenon.

OUR PROPOSAL

To begin this chapter we have chosen to include information relating to a small pilot study that was undertaken by Louise Mullins in September 2015.

To begin with, Louise sought the permission of her supervisor and regulating body, as well as from a small private research committee, to investigate the prevalence of obsessive thoughts and compulsive behaviours, as characteristics within individuals diagnosed with at least one mental health disorder.

The ethical approval was based on her ability to obtain informed consent through an anonymous online survey, and to offer any individuals taking part an appropriate 'debrief', and emotional support if required. The questions also had to be worded so as not to show bias in supporting the theory, nor to possibly trigger such vulnerable individuals. The rigorous process of approval identified two possible issues.

Firstly, as a therapist and researcher it would not be advisable for Louise to offer emotional support to individuals to which she was unlikely to be able to meet on a one-to-one basis, or could possibly be an individual whom she knows personally or professionally.

Secondly, it is difficult to obtain informed consent from an individual who is taking part in a study anonymously.

For these two reasons the study was approved on

the basis that these two possible confounding variables were unlikely to cause an issue in an online survey.

The decision to investigate the phenomenon via an online survey, was to enable a large pool of participants to be involved, and for a wide variation in volunteers age, gender, race, culture, religion, social class, dis(ability), diagnosis - Something Louise thought was important. The inclusion of anyone in the study was intended to offer a wide variation in responses, whilst enabling a quantifiable method of data to be collected.

The study was based on the theories of Cognitive Behavioural Disorder and Habitual Behaviour Disorder. The survey contained nine multiple choice questions. Respondents were given the opportunity to disclose their mental health diagnosis for question ten, should they choose to do so.

The questions were placed into several categories of enquiry (see appendix 1 for a complete copy of the survey). These included: Negative thoughts, negative feelings, actions, consequences, compulsive behaviour, OCD and addiction.

All of the questions were quantifiable, in that they were statistically relevant. However the final question, where participants were able to disclose their mental health diagnosis, also sought a qualitative method to analysis (aimed at seeking a subjective answer). You can view appendix 3 for the findings of the qualitative part of the study.

The dependent variable was the percentage of respondent's ratings (the variable that is quantifiable). The independent variables were the number of respondents taking part, and the amount of questions answered by those respondents.

Self-reports/disclosures of a psychological diagnosis were used within the qualitative analysis after the results of the quantitative study were calculated.

The hypothesis was that more respondents will show characteristics of obsessive thoughts and compulsive behaviours than will not, for all psychological diagnoses.

Habitual Behaviour Disorder theory was used to determine whether such characteristics were more prevalent within individuals diagnosed with OCD or addiction. Thus two of the questions posed asked whether or not the individual taking part had ever been, or was currently, diagnosed with OCD or addiction.

Although the statistics are currently being monitored and the results are being updated regularly (the survey is still available online), the first set of results look promising (see appendix 2).

From 156 respondents for the initial stage of the analysis (the first day of survey operation), the data collected from 100 of the participant-responses was analysed. Eighty-nine of the respondents chose to answer question ten.

Before we proceed with an explanation of the results we wish to explain why we have chosen to take an informal approach to writing about our findings.

Firstly, as previously stated, this book is intended for anyone with a personal or professional interest in obsessive thoughts and compulsive behaviours to understand.

Secondly, we wish to invite you into the research processes used by practitioners, as though you have no prior understanding of the data collection, analysis, or the calculation of statistics involved in the research process.

In order for such information to make sense to students, teachers, practitioners, clients and researchers alike, we have deliberately presented a copy of the questionnaire (questions and answers), results and findings, in an informal, easy to comprehend format. We want anyone to be able to understand them. We hope to ignite the possibility that such a study is replicated. And for this, we need to present the study as an introduction to psychological research, and not as an advanced investigation.

The findings from the study suggest several important factors which may validate the significance of our theory, and thus, support our approach.

Firstly, there was a statistical significance between negative thoughts (questions 2 and 3), feelings (question 4), and consequences (question 6). This data was calculated according to the comparative difference of 29-32% (the lowest total difference between percentages as recorded within the data). Put simply, if any of the answers to the questions (yes/often) scored a total percentage above at least 29% (29-32%) it would be considered statistically significant.

However, let's not get carried away - such a significance between examples did not correlate strongly with negative answers (No/not at all).

For example, within the data there was no significant difference between individuals who answered negatively (no/not at all) to question 1 (negative thoughts), 5 (actions), or to those relating to a diagnosis of OCD (question 8) or addiction (question 9): Although the correlation between individuals who expressed their behaviour as 'compulsive', did match those who did not (34.00%).

Secondly, there was also a positive correlation between individuals diagnosed with a psychological disorder, who answered positively to questions relating to negative thoughts, feelings, and behaviour, compared to those who were not (399-192= 207). This is calculated according to the total amount of individuals who answered these four questions (399), minus the total positive answers to the questions posed (yes/often) which were 192. We then subtract this number from the other (399-192) to calculate our answer (207).

Thirdly, obsessive thoughts and compulsive behaviours were present characteristics within individuals who had a current diagnosis of one or more psychological disorder(s).

When adding the data obtained from question ten, where participants were asked to disclose their mental health diagnosis (if they so wished), it was found that those individuals with a current diagnosis of depression or anxiety, expressed obsessive thoughts and compulsive behaviours at a higher level than we would expect, if we were to compare them to individuals with any other mental health diagnosis. Those individuals with a diagnosis of depression presented the highest levels of obsessive thoughts and compulsive behaviour (59.63%), compared to those with a diagnosis of anxiety (48.06%).

Finally, although not showing a significant difference *within* the study (compared to other diagnosable psychological disorders), *between* individuals without a psychological diagnosis (participants with a diagnosis for PTSD (14.24%), OCD (9.79%), stress (8.9%), and addiction (8.9%) a significant correlation was found (above the comparative difference rate of 29-32%).

These findings suggest that not only are obsessive thoughts and compulsive behaviours present characteristics in individuals diagnosed with six of the many psychological disorders currently recognised, but that these findings require further study into comparisons between individuals who do not have a prior or current diagnosable psychological disorder.

The results appear to support a theory for obsessive thoughts and compulsive behaviours, and suggest that the prevalence of these characteristics is researchable: Thus, Cognitive Behavioural Disorder could be an assessable, diagnosable, and treatable disorder.

We propose that the future research of this theory and possible disorder is replicable, and believe that such a theory can advance current policies and procedures in the advancement of knowledge towards mental health problems.

We hope that you have enjoyed reading this book

and we invite you to enter the debate on whether our theory could advance current knowledge on obsessive thoughts and compulsive behaviours as related to mental health.

We believe that the research we have already carried out is replicable and that such investigation will aid our current understanding of mental health disorders.

We hope that whether you are a student, teacher, practitioner or researcher we have ignited a passion within you to answer many of the questions we have posed throughout this book. That you will now be spurred on to raise this debate within your own professional field/university, begin to ask questions that seek to address the issue of CBD and the use of CBT to treat the disorder, and to begin your own research into testing the phenomenon.

Over the page you will be able to contact either author in relation to the subject of this book, and we hope that you do.

REFERENCES

CHAPTER ONE

Page 25 and 26:
Goodman, W. (2013) 'What causes Obsessive Compulsive Disorder (OCD)?' *Psych Central* [Online]. Retrieved on 15th September 2015, from: http://psychcentral.com/lib/what-causes-obsessive-compulsive-disorder-ocd/

Page 23:
Janet, P. (1902) Cited by Goodman, W. 'What causes Obsessive Compulsive Disorder (OCD)?' *Psych Central* [Online]. Retrieved on 15th September 2015, from: http://psychcentral.com/lib/what-causes-obsessive-compulsive-disorder-ocd/

APPENDIX 1

CBD Questionnaire

The aim of this questionnaire is to find out how negative thoughts and behaviours affect individuals with a diagnosis of any mental health disorder.

There are just 10 questions for you to answer which should take you less than two minutes. Please answer each question as honestly as you can.

Thank you in advance for choosing to take part.

The information we receive is completely anonymous and will assist the future research of the relationship between our thoughts and behaviour. This survey was produced as part of the study towards a new theory. By taking part in this survey you are assisting the researcher in investigating a possible connection between over-thinking and behaviour.

Louise Mullins (MNCS)

Psychological Therapist & Trainee Clinical Forensic Psychologist

1. Since your diagnosis, how often do you experience negative or unpleasant thoughts? (These could be internal negative comments, such as: I'm useless, I'm to blame, I'm stupid, I'm fat etc. or thoughts of harming oneself or harming others)

Several times a day

At least once a day

Once or twice a week

2. Since your diagnosis have you ever experienced intrusive memories or recurrent thoughts that you find difficult to manage? (These could be remembering events that have happened, imagining events that could happen or intrusive thoughts that accompany negative feelings such as: low mood, loss of appetite, increased or decreased awareness of your surroundings, and considering self-harm, suicide or harming another individual)

Often

Sometimes

Not at all

3. When you are thinking, remembering, imagining or considering things do you ever feel that you do so too much? (Do you ever question whether your thoughts are too negative, that you are spending too much time thinking them or that they

are obsessive?)

Yes

Sometimes

No

4. Do you often find that negative feelings accompany your thoughts? (Here we mean negative thoughts)

Yes

Sometimes

No

5. Do you ever act on the feelings associated with your thoughts? (For instance, if you have a diagnosis of OCD, do you ever act on your impulse to clean because you cannot stop thinking about it, and find the feelings too difficult to ignore) Please note this is just an example.

Yes

Sometimes

No

6. Do you feel that your actions ever have negative consequences? (For instance, if you have

been diagnosed with PTSD, do you ever avoid certain activities, or react to situations that you later regret?) Please note that this is just an example.

Yes

Sometimes

No

7. Have you ever felt that your actions as a result of your feelings and thoughts are compulsive in nature? (That is that you behave on impulse, without thought? That your actions are 'automatic'?)

Yes

Sometimes

No

8. Have you ever suffered from or been diagnosed with OCD (Obsessive Compulsive Disorder)?

Yes

No

9. Have you ever suffered from or been diagnosed with an addiction? (To anything)

Yes

No

10. If you feel comfortable to do so please tell us what you have been diagnosed with? (For instance, stress, anxiety, depression, PTSD, depression, bipolar, addiction, OCD, phobia, eating disorder etc.)

APPENDIX 2

Question	Answer	Percentage	Total responses
1	1	34.69%	34
	2	36.73%	36
	3	28.57%	28
2	1	47.47%	47
	2	41.41%	41
	3	11.11%	11
3	1	48.00%	48
	2	31.00%	31
	3	21.00%	21
4	1	61.00%	61
	2	25.00%	25
	3	14.00%	14
5	1	31.31%	31

Question	Answer	Percentage	Total responses
	2	40.40%	40
6	3	28.28%	28
	1	51.00%	51
	2	32.00%	32
7	3	17.00%	17
	1	34.00%	34
	2	32.00%	32
8	3	34.00%	34
	1	15.00%	15
9	2	85.00%	85
	1	21.00%	21
1	2	79.00%	79

APPENDIX 3

Diagnosis	Total Percentage	Probability Value (that the results are not related to chance)	Statistical difference between comparison
Depression	59.63%	29.22%	32.83%
Anxiety	48.06%	57.68%	64.81%
PTSD	14.24%	406.0%	456.25%
OCD	9.79%	631.09%	709.09%
Stress	8.9%	703.01%	790%
Addiction	8.9%	703.01%	790%
Eating disorder	7.12%	901.25%	1012.5%
Personality Disorder	5.34%	1231.16%	1483.3%
Bipolar	4.45%	1495.2%	1780%
Other	8.9%	703.01%	790%

KEEP IN TOUCH WITH LOUISE

Website:
https://louisemullins2010.wix.com/author

Goodreads:
https://www.goodreads.com/LouiseMullinsAuthor

Facebook:
https://www.facebook.com/LouiseMullinsAuthor

Twitter:
https://twitter.com/MullinsAuthor

LinkedIn:
https://uk.linkedin.com/in/louisemullinsauthor

Wordpress:
https://louisemullinsauthor.wordpress.com

KEEP IN TOUCH WITH SUE

Website:
https://www.thumbsupprogramme.co.uk

Facebook:
https://www.facebook.com/thumbsupprogramme

Twitter:
https://twitter.com/thumbsupprog

www.ingramcontent.com/pod-product-compliance
Lightning Source LLC
Chambersburg PA
CBHW071238280526
45787CB00002B/980